The RAND Corporation—a nonprofit corporation formed

*To further and promote scientific, educational, and charitable purposes, all for the public welfare and security of the United States of America.*
—Articles of Incorporation

# THE RAND CORPORATION

*THE FIRST FIFTEEN YEARS*

NOVEMBER 1963

SANTA MONICA, CALIFORNIA

# Preface

When a research concept called *Air Force Project* RAND emerged in 1946, it brought together a small group of persons interested in the nation's security. This group evolved into an organization that in 1948 became The RAND Corporation: a nonprofit institution which seeks rational, scientific approaches to problems important to the national interest.

In retrospect, RAND has filled a special need of history and circumstances. The way that need has been filled, and the response to it—the development both of RAND itself and of the niche for service that the Corporation and the circumstances of our times have created—may be of considerable interest for the future. Accordingly, on RAND's fifteenth anniversary, a review of its history, goals, and record seems appropriate.

# This is RAND

THE RAND CORPORATION IS DEDICATED TO THE TASK OF contributing to the public welfare, and specifically to the nation's security. It seeks to create an environment in which talented men and women, trained in various disciplines—the natural sciences, mathematics, economics, and the other social sciences—can explore together many kinds of problems and their solutions in a wide range of areas affecting the continuing security and welfare of America. RAND's investigations range from narrow and specific technical subjects, such as those involving the development of a new technology, to consideration of broad strategic concepts. The Corporation has no laboratories in the usual sense. It does not manufacture, does not normally engage in design or evaluation of specific products, and does not manage or direct any operations but its own.

An over-all view of RAND is difficult to present, in part *Sponsors* because of the great diversity of its interests and its skills, and the range of its sponsors. The Air Force is its principal sponsor, but its work is also supported by the Office of the Secretary of Defense, the Atomic Energy Commission, the National Aeronautics and Space Administration, the National Institutes of Health, and other government agencies. Nongovernmental sponsors of RAND research have included The Ford Foundation, The Rockefeller Foundation, and The Carnegie Corporation. In addition, RAND undertakes 1 research, supported by its own funds, in various fields of public interest.

*Objectives*        In 1946 the Project RAND objective was stated as "a program of study and research on the broad subject of intercontinental warfare other than surface," to include recommendations of "preferred techniques and instrumentalities" to the Army Air Forces. This basic objective, with minor modifications, still governs The RAND Corporation's work for the Air Force, although the study of intercontinental warfare in this context is interpreted in the broadest sense as including the pursuit of the twin objectives of decreasing the probability of thermonuclear or other war and of stemming or reversing the advance of Communism—the task of seeking peace but preserving freedom. Moreover, the search for preferred instrumentalities to these ends has led to research programs of unexpected scope and diversity.

For other RAND sponsors, the fields of study often differ from those for the Air Force, but the search for "preferred" techniques, instrumentalities, and policies is central to them all.

There is a deliberate attempt to keep the atmosphere at RAND informal and unrestrictive, to provide a climate suitable for creative work. In this, as in all its efforts, achievement falls short of aspiration. Yet the attempt has been sufficiently successful that the Corporation has been described as "a university without students." A Harvard professor, commenting on a sabbatic year spent at RAND, wrote:

> During the year before this book went to press I was uniquely located to receive stimulation, provocation, advice, comment, disagreement, encouragement, and education. . . . As a collection of people RAND is superb . . . but RAND is more than a collection of people; it is a social organism characterized by intellect, imagination, and good humor.

*Organization*   ·   The RAND technical staff is subdivided into departments which, for the most part, are formed along lines of professional 2   skills: Aero-Astronautics, Computer Sciences, Cost Analysis,

Economics, Electronics, Logistics, Mathematics, Physics, Planetary Sciences, Social Science, and System Operations. These compartments are not to be taken too literally: skills of mathematics and physics are found in the Economics Department, chemistry and sociology both exist in Mathematics, and philosophy is represented in several departments. Diversity is the rule; each department differs from all the others in structure, organization, degree of direction exercised by the department head, and involvement in RAND-wide multidisciplinary projects. For one department the organization chart makes a complicated design dissected by intricate patterns of lines of authority; for another, the chart resolves to a simple listing of names in alphabetical order.

An Air Force officer, stationed at RAND, wrote of this unique environment:

Here at RAND, men trained in various disciplines may discover new results in basic science, develop new analytical techniques, produce inventions. They look into the future, project trends, imagine contingencies. They seek preferred courses of action, preferred concepts, doctrine, and tactics, and preferred allocations of resources.

Because of the diversity of skills and knowledge required to cope with current and future problems of national security, and because of the interest which all on the research staff share in the solution of these problems, an organization like RAND represents one (rare) device for overcoming the increasing compartmentalization and specialization of knowledge.

There have been no boundaries to individual areas of research. If analyses are to be useful, to have breadth and originality, many staff members of many diverse skills must contribute to them, and often in ways unforeseen in the beginning of an analysis. To work together productively, the physicist must know some political science, the political scientist must know some physics, and both must have the fullest possible knowledge of the problem they are attacking and the context in which it arises.

At RAND, contributions to solutions of problems come from unexpected corners of the building. A mathematical tool developed for use in economic problems turns out to be useful in treating problems of space vehicle navigation. A technique devised for theoretical work in biology proves useful in control engineering. An economist, not working on the project, calls attention to some unnoticed implications in defense against ballistic missiles. Any single RAND project, for example, may be staffed by, say, four men— each of a different academic discipline—but able to use instantly the consulting services of ten times this number of staff members.

Formal attempts to distill wisdom from the efforts of two or more thinkers, at RAND, as everywhere, are usually awkward and painful; for thinking is essentially a solitary process. An idea is generated, an essay is written by an individual, not by a committee. But at RAND every possible effort is made to enable this creating individual to draw strength and inspiration from as rich an environment as can be architected. Every effort is made to give him the chance to sharpen his ideas upon his colleagues as he addresses problems whose many facets may demand a greater variety of skills than any one individual possesses, or can possess.

RAND has grown to include today some 1100 employees. Approximately half of them are professionals, in fields ranging from aerodynamics and anthropology to sociology and statistics. The increase in the complexity of its work, of which this diversity of personnel offers one index, has paralleled the increasing complexity of national security problems which confront our country. When RAND's work began, the United States had a monopoly on nuclear weapons and on the means of their delivery. Now four great nations possess these capabilities; and more may enter the lists. With this diffusion, many military problems have changed. Moreover, such problems as those of Berlin, Korea, Cuba, and Vietnam cannot be resolved merely by nuclear weapons. The ever-accelerating growth of scientific knowledge and technical change, and the imperatives of national survival in a nuclear age, demand that we make highly informed and highly effective use of our resources and exercise the broadest wisdom in our policy choices.

What follows deals more fully with the background and nature of The RAND Corporation and, in particular, with some of the work it has done.

# How RAND Began

In world war ii, the united states was ultimately able to contribute significantly to victory only because our allies could bear the brunt of early battles. We also learned that it takes precious time to reduce to practice new weapons that may be finally decisive. Radar had been proposed in the late 1920's; the uses of nuclear fission had been hinted in 1939; the theories behind the computing bombsight were known earlier than the propaganda of Adolf Hitler.

A further lesson learned in World War II was that new weapons demand new tactics, and may even require the agonizing reappraisal of basic concepts of strategy and policy. The V-bombs that emerged from Germany's laboratories in the last days of the Third Reich almost destroyed London. Had they been available three years earlier they might well have decided the war in Europe. The advent of the atom bomb soon called into question almost every facet of conventional military doctrine.

In postwar years the United States has undertaken vastly expanded responsibilities involving the well-being of much of the world. We have found our knowledge and skills and wisdom in international affairs all to be seriously deficient for the task. Such lessons of peace and war continually underline the need for new concepts not only of military forces and weapons, but also of strategy and policy planning generally.

To meet some of these needs in the postwar years, it was clearly important to preserve part of the scientific corps that had been mobilized during the war to develop the atom bomb, the proximity fuze, radar, and many other devices. That work had been done through emergency organizations, such as the Manhattan District and the Office of Scientific Research and Development, and through special working arrangements with universities and industry. With victory, most scientists were anxious to return to former pursuits, and it was imperative that some cohesion be maintained among them.

Various settings were considered after the war for a permanent research organization of a new kind. Neither the military establishment nor a civilian governmental organization seemed likely to provide the environment needed. Government analyses are made under a necessary pressure to solve the problems of here-and-now; the need to insure policy coordination makes difficult a wide-ranging examination of contingencies. Such analyses are likely to be constricted. A university center would have the asset of first-rate talent; however, the difficulties of security classification and of doing interdisciplinary work, and the near absence of a well-developed body of thought and community of scholars dedicated to the study of national security as an analytic field, all argued against setting up the new organization on a university campus. So, under the circumstances, it was proposed that the organization be temporarily housed and administered by an industrial contractor experienced in the ways of research.

One of those most keenly interested in developing the organization was General H. H. Arnold, Commanding General of the Army Air Forces. In late 1945, he suggested and effected a contract between the Army Air Forces and the Douglas Aircraft Company. This contract came to be called Project RAND (for "research and development"). General Arnold ordered that $10 million be allocated for the project—enough to underwrite operations until the new organization would be able to prove itself.

The project was set up in May of 1946 as a virtually autono- *Project* mous department of Douglas, and a number of Douglas staff *RAND* members were invited to join the activity. F. R. Collbohm, Assist- ant to the Vice President, Engineering, who had been actively involved in formulating the idea of RAND, was chosen to direct it and has served as its chief executive officer ever since. Important Air Force policy guidelines for Project RAND were established: its independence was to be guaranteed and its research was to be long-range in nature; it was to have a large measure of freedom in determining its own research program. It was to receive Air Force intelligence and planning information and, in due course, make reports and recommendations as warranted by research. These would be available to Air Force planners for such use as they saw fit.

These Air Force policies, and the guarantee of long-term initial support that was given, made possible the growth and development of Project RAND and The RAND Corporation.

# The Early Years

ONE OF THE FIRST STAFF MEMBERS HAS DESCRIBED SOME OF the small problems that arose in the initial environment of RAND:

> We had to fit into existing molds. For example, the Douglas Company did not have a job description for a philosopher. By reading the job-salary table backward, we discovered that he was a Design Specialist A. This solved a RAND problem, but may have created some for the aircraft industry, and also left some personal ones. If he met someone who identified himself as being from, say, United Shoe Machinery, it was only polite to respond "I am with Douglas Aircraft." The next question might be, "How's business?" Our philosopher, of course, knew nothing about how business was. In professional circles it was worse. Academic people are like gypsies, so if you haven't seen a man for a few years, it is natural to ask, "Where are you now?" The statement "Douglas Aircraft" might be met with "How quaint!" Then, of course, people wanted to know what he did there, and he was free to say only "Philosophy"... you can imagine the rest.
>
> The matter of hours of work were—and are yet—a substantial trial. Academic people have irregular habits and have never taken kindly to the eight-to-five routine. We had one man who rarely showed up before two o'clock, and another who almost never went home—this, mind you, in an organization where they physically locked the doors at about five, and kept them locked until about eight in the morning. They changed this for us, so people could work nights and weekends....

*Satellites*

A sampling of the studies of that period is illuminating. The first major task, suggested by the Air Force in 1946, was to study the feasibility and military usefulness of an artificial earth satellite

8

—an object then of interest primarily to science-fiction writers. The conclusion was that a primitive satellite could be launched by 1952. In a letter transmitting a report on this subject to the Air Force, RAND wrote that it considered

the construction of a satellite to be technically feasible, the problems associated with instrumentation and guidance being more difficult of solution than those of building the vehicle itself. The scientific data which a satellite can secure and transmit to earth are extremely valuable and the vehicle has important military uses in connection with mapping and reconnaissance, as a communications relay station, and in association with long-range missiles.

The report also foresaw the political importance of a satellite. Air Force Secretary Zuckert recently told the American Astronautical Society,

One of the first RAND studies, delivered to the Air Materiel Command at Wright Field early in 1946, was so prophetic that I would like to read you an excerpt. The report observed that: "Since mastery of the elements is a reliable index of material progress, the nation which first makes significant achievements in space travel will be acknowledged as the world leader in both military and scientific techniques. To visualize the impact on the world, one can imagine the consternation and admiration that would be felt here if the U.S. were to discover suddenly that some other nation had already put up a successful satellite."

That 1946 report, *Preliminary Design of an Experimental Earth-Circling Spaceship*, estimated the state of the art, not the nation's interest in the topic. But the findings were the foundation of a continuing program of research which, through the years, was to yield hundreds of reports on space technology, including meteorological satellites, planetary explorations, and ballistic and glide rockets. Studies of open Soviet space literature led to an educated guess in mid-1957 as to when Sputnik I would be launched. It missed by only two weeks.

In these early years, RAND also studied a wide-ranging variety of subjects. They included, among others, ramjets and rocket engines for strategic weapons, boron and other high-energy fuels, the statistical theory of radar detection, atmospheric physics, the theory of games, econometrics, air defense, nuclear propulsion, metal fatigue, optimal design of structures for military aircraft, bomber and fighter design, air-traffic control, and high-energy radiation. A quantitative RAND analysis of the gains in range that could be realized by in-flight refueling of aircraft during this period led to the practical adoption of this technique by the Air Force for its long-range missions.

A new lightweight metal, titanium, previously unusable in flight structures, was brought to industrial technology during this period. RAND-supported experimental research at Battelle Memorial Institute was the first to produce titanium in wrought form. Its high strength-to-weight ratio, particularly at high temperatures, made it appear promising for use in the high-speed flight vehicles then contemplated. From that small beginning, a major metallurgical industry has grown.

The physical sciences are inadequate in themselves for an effective solution of major problems of national security, for the physical aspects of security problems cannot be separated from their international political and economic aspects. Force and diplomacy, military action and political maneuver, are entwined as rarely before in American history. For these reasons, RAND sought early the services of men outside the physical sciences.

To establish working relations with experts in the fields of the behavioral sciences, and to suggest a research program there, a conference was convened in 1947. Some of the participants in it were to form the nucleus of the Social Science and Economics departments at RAND. At this conference the philosopher, the psychologist, and the political scientist joined the sociologist and the economist in discussing contributions that the sciences of man might make to national security research. U.S. goals and values, decisionmaking in the U.S.S.R., economic sources of international friction, foreign economic assistance—these and other topics

10

were discussed during the six-day conference. Warren Weaver, then of The Rockefeller Foundation, described the tone both of the conference and of RAND in his opening remarks:

I assume that everyone here is devoted to what can broadly be called the rational life. He believes fundamentally that there is something to this business of having some knowledge, and some experience, and some insight, and some analysis of problems, as compared with living in a state of ignorance, superstition, and drifting-into-whatever-may-come. . . . I think that we are interested, not in war, but in peace. . . . I assume that every person in this room is desperately dedicated to the ideals of democracy, and to so running our own business, so cleaning our own house, and so improving our own relations with the rest of the world that the value of those ideals in which we believe becomes thereby evident.

# The Corporation

By 1948 THE VALIDITY OF THE BASIC CONCEPT SEEMED ESTAB-
lished and RAND was ready to stand on its own feet. Accordingly,
steps were taken to form a more appropriate organization, and in
November The RAND Corporation came into being. The Corporation, independent and nonprofit, has no stock and no stock-
holders. None of its assets may inure to the benefit of any individual. All must be used for research or other public purposes.

The Corporation is governed by its Board of Trustees, representing the public interest. Its members bring wide experience
from business and industry, and from the natural and social
sciences. The Board appoints the officers of the Corporation and
establishes the general policies which guide them. It reviews the
fiscal affairs of the Corporation, its relations with client agencies,
and periodically samples its research.

*Financing*    H. Rowan Gaither, Jr., a distinguished attorney who played
a leading role in forming the Corporation, wrote the Articles of
Incorporation, and helped enlist outstanding men to serve on
RAND's Board of Trustees. He also helped to raise the initial
working capital of $1,000,000—through a $100,000 loan from
the nascent Ford Foundation, and bank lines of credit of
$900,000. The Ford Foundation later increased its loan to $1
million and in 1952 converted the loan to a grant for research.
12    Gaither served as Board Chairman until his death in 1961, except

for a one-year term served by William Webster. He was succeeded by the present chairman, Frank Stanton.

The budget of the Corporation for the first year was $3,750,000. In the fifteenth year it was $20,660,000, representing an average growth of about 10 per cent per year. These funds came largely from the United States Air Force, under the contract known as Project RAND. In the current year, RAND's fifteenth, research for other government sponsors and research supported by grants or from the Corporation's own funds account for 30 per cent of its activities.

The material Air Force support for Project RAND has been vital to the Corporation. But the conditions under which that support has been given have had even more to do with the Corporation's success than the amount and consistency of the support alone imply. The breadth and generality of the contract has permitted the Corporation—and individual researchers within it—to explore new and often unconventional ideas without first getting explicit approval from a hierarchy of corporate and government administrators and committees. Thus, viable ideas get an early and effective start; less effective ones can be eliminated early, and with little cost. Such an environment is highly attractive to creative individuals, for it is one where it matters deeply that they be creative. Some persons seem to feel that "research freedom" is a tired cliché, perhaps irresponsible license. It is in fact the basis of The RAND Corporation's progress, and it stems largely from the enlightened permissiveness of the Air Force's management of the Project RAND contract.

Having a variety of clients is more important than the dollars or percentages suggest. They offer the only way to fill gaps in RAND experience or information, which leads to a better understanding of national security problems. A program of wide scope enhances RAND's work, redounding to the benefit of the Corporation's sponsors and all users of RAND research.     13

# The Work of RAND

W<small>E ATTEMPT NOW TO SHOW THE KINDS OF STUDIES DONE AT</small>
RAND—with apologies both to the readers and to the researchers,
because it is impossible to satisfy either group. A complete
catalog of studies would be almost endless (hundreds of titles).
It would be unreadable, and uninformative. Therefore we must
concentrate on a few representative ones, trying to say something significant about each in a very brief compass. Most researchers will find that this necessary approach slights their
work, and most readers will find that the topics selected exceed
the limits of their interests. It may please both groups to learn
that the compilers of this review are unhappy, too!

Also, this is not in any sense a catalog of "accomplishments." Any such catalog would be highly suspect, for it is
extremely difficult to assign credit. When a route on which RAND
has thrown some light is taken, it is seldom clear how much
credit is due. On some occasions it may indeed have been the
prime mover; on others, a catalytic agent; and in many cases it
has added one more voice (or several diverse ones) to a many
sided debate that illuminated various facets of a problem. The
effect of RAND, then, can only be inferred, rather than measured,
because it is embedded in a complex of affairs to which countless
14  organizations and individuals have contributed.

Such a review of studies at RAND may begin with a glance *Policy*
at the continuing dialogue on the concepts of national security *Research*
which takes place there; at the discussions inside and outside the
halls of RAND that attempt to throw light on the basic problems
of how to stay alive and free. Some of the topics of this debate
are suggested by a RAND author:

> . . . our rejection of preventive war has committed us to a deterrent
> strategy, and consequently . . . we must be willing to pay the price to make
> it work . . . a great nation which has forsworn preventive war *must* devote
> much of its military energies to cutting down drastically the advantage that
> the enemy can derive from hitting first by surprise attack. This . . . means
> above all guaranteeing through various forms of protection the survival of
> the retaliatory force under attack. . . .

. . .

> The second basic principle of action for the United States is to provide
> a real and substantial capability for coping with limited and local aggression
> by local application of force. This is to avoid our finding ourselves some day
> in a dilemma where we must either accept defeat on a local issue of great
> importance, or else resort to a kind of force which may be intrinsically
> inappropriate and which may critically increase the risk of total war.

. . .

> In view of the danger that limited war can erupt into total war . . . [we]
> have to accept the idea that the methods of limiting the use of force cannot
> be dictated by us according to our conceptions of our own convenience.
> Among the compromises with our presumed convenience which we have to
> be prepared to consider is the possible abjuration of nuclear weapons in
> limited war. Obviously we have to be prepared also to fight with them, but
> that is very different from not being prepared to fight without them. . . .

. . .

> The third principle follows simply from taking *seriously* the fact that
> the danger of total war is real and finite. Provision must be made for the
> saving of life on a vast scale. . . .

. . .

> The strategic air ascendancy which determines the outcome is itself
> decided by the questions, (a) Who strikes first? (b) With what degree of

surprise? (c) Against what preparations made by the other side to insure that its retaliatory force will survive and return the fire? It is . . . conceivable that the way in which these and related issues are resolved will mean that no real ascendancy is established with the first exchange of blows. If so, what follows will be . . . an extraordinarily destructive yet quick contest to determine who retains exclusive capability for yet further nuclear destruction.

. . .

The unsolved problem of modern total war (if it should come) is that of how to stop it, quickly, once it is decided. It is tantamount to negotiating complete disarmament with a 24-hour deadline, or less.

It is worth noting that RAND does not by any means speak with one voice on these matters. There is no attempt to force a consensus, for strong disagreements throw light on many aspects of a problem.

\*     \*     \*

*Bases*     Analysis involves many things. It may begin with the basic and ever-recurrent question: What is the real problem? That query often leads to reformulation of the question to be addressed, and eventually to the solution of problems not originally perceived. Thus a study of overseas bases, conceived as a logistics exercise, turned out to involve directly and critically the nation's over-all deterrent capability. The study broadened to include relations with allied nations; comparisons of aircraft and missile characteristics; vulnerability of U.S. cities, and of domestic bases of the Strategic Air Command; and the responses of SAC in the event of enemy attack. The findings contributed to an Air Force decision to revise its strategic air base structure, which, according to an Air Staff estimate, saved $1 billion in proposed installation costs while maintaining the same strategic capability. The work also stimulated research on a bomb-alarm system, airborne alert, long-endurance aircraft, and base-hardening and protective construction.

16

Another example concerns a basic research project, with results that called for immediate application. In 1950 a team of psychologists began to study how men and machines work together; in particular, how men respond to conditions of stress. They simulated an Air Defense Direction Center, and used college students as experimental subjects. The students came to understand their duties by "walking through" a series of increasingly complicated situations involving "air raids" plus normal air traffic. The results of these tests became available immediately, so that the students could revise their procedures in the light of this information. Soon they were able to handle heavier traffic loads than experienced crews were carrying in real situations. The Air Defense Command asked that a similar experiment be run with military crews, and similar improvements in handling followed. Thus a research program on patterns of behavior under stress led to the development of a valuable method for training Air Force personnel.

In 1953 the Air Force asked RAND to put this training system into operation throughout the Air Defense Command. A special group, the System Development Division, was set up within RAND for that purpose. This Division subsequently undertook to provide computer programs for the SAGE system—the then new semiautomatic air defense control system—and to develop training methods for SAGE crews. Because it differed in purpose and was twice the size of the rest of RAND, the Division was "spun off" in 1957 as the System Development Corporation; at the request of the Air Force it was organized as an independent nonprofit corporate entity.

A system of a very different sort was the subject of another study. It involved the effects of unintentional radio signal interference on the performance of weapons. Radio-equipped taxis and ham operators were known occasionally to interfere with missile launchings, but no systematic analysis had been made    17

of such effects of various items of military electronic equipment
on one another. The results of the research led to design changes
in weapons and control systems, and to better coordination of
frequency allocations among users and manufacturers of equipment. The Defense Department now maintains an Electronic
Compatibility Analysis Center; RAND helped set it in operation,
and continues to assist in its program.

*   *   *

RAND has investigated other means for limiting war damage
should deterrence fail. Prominent among them is civil defense.
Much can be done to alleviate the consequences of even total
war, if all kinds of defense, including passive defense, are used.

*Nuclear*      In 1950 RAND's research in the field of nuclear physics was
*Weapons*   expanded as a result of a contract with the Atomic Energy
Commission. Since then the Corporation has worked closely with
the laboratories of the AEC on many aspects of nuclear weapons
—from reports of the early 1950's on the hydrodynamics of
nuclear explosions, to recent work on the detection of explosions at very high altitudes. The thermonuclear weapons research
authorized by the President early in 1950 resulted, by late 1951,
in an idea for a practical bomb design. When the AEC reported
this development to the President, the Joint Chiefs, and the
military services, RAND was ready with a detailed analysis of the
potential effects of the new weapons and their political and
military implications.

RAND has attempted to understand better the effects of
nuclear weapons: on enemy targets, on defensive installations,
on offensive delivery vehicles, and on other nuclear weapons.
RAND's nuclear-effects studies have provided knowledge for use
18   in estimating military and civilian vulnerabilities; for establish-

ing technical standards for sheltering from the effects of blast, heat, and radiation; for the design of nuclear test programs and interpretation of test results; for improving the methods for detecting nuclear tests; and for devising ways to disarm incoming missiles. RAND's mathematical models permit predictions to be made of fallout, and of the radiation effects from nuclear explosions. These have been used widely by government agencies; for example, by the AEC in scheduling test shots in Nevada.

In its studies of nuclear fallout, the Corporation drew upon its earlier research on the physics of the upper atmosphere. The *Meteorology* 1957 report, *Close-in Fallout*, describing the physics of fallout from nuclear devices and methods for its prediction, was distributed by the U.S. Weather Bureau to stations having a potential fallout prediction job, and RAND has continued to advise the North American Air Defense Command and other agencies on this subject.

*       *       *

A fundamental consideration in satellite and missile flight is the environment in the upper atmosphere, or "near space." The first RAND report in this area, issued in 1948, presented an analysis of the temperature, pressure, and density of the atmosphere extending to about 10,000 miles "altitude." For some years this was the standard reference in its field, and the basis of many essential calculations, including re-entry of satellites and missiles. Work on the physics and meteorology of the upper atmosphere has continued, and the scientific literature attests to RAND's contributions to our understanding of the circulations and energy sources in the stratosphere and above, the air densities and compositions at satellite altitudes, the theory of the radiation belts, the formation of auroras, and the earth's magnetic field and its changes.                                                                              19

*Cost*
*Analysis*

Cost analysis as developed at RAND involves economics, statistics, and engineering, as well as detailed estimates of future environments and operations. How much will it cost to develop and operate a new air defense system? a communication satellite system? a supersonic transport? These are not simple problems in cost accounting. The enormous costs of modern systems over the long term must be estimated realistically, because they are important factors in choosing wisely from modern technology. The real costs of a weapon system, in fact, greatly exceed the original costs of procuring the weapons themselves. They involve the total resources for operating the system over the years, including the required manpower, necessary new facilities, transportation, support equipment, and so on. Using RAND techniques, military planners can project into the future the economic implications of today's decisions—not perfectly, but better than before.

The Air Force began to make use of RAND's cost analysis and fiscal planning methods ten years ago. It was already using this management tool when Secretary McNamara and Defense Comptroller Hitch introduced it throughout the military establishment in 1961. It has led to concurrent planning, programming, and budgeting, and makes possible an integrated view of the entire Defense Department as a functional unit with respect to activities, missions, and the instrumentalities proposed for carrying out these missions. Industry has shown wide interest in the methods, and variants of them may be adopted by other federal agencies.

\*     \*     \*

*Logistics*

Large dollar economies can often be realized through changes of logistics policies. RAND has undertaken much research in this area. Analyses of past procurement programs and of current supply and maintenance procedures have revealed ways

20

of cutting costs and, simultaneously, of increasing effectiveness. Studies have been and are being made of military air transport, spare parts procurement and stockage policies, data processing, automatic checkout equipment, logistic support of conflicts in distant locales, with special attention to our need for overseas bases, and techniques for support of new missile systems. To cite one example in this field, a study of storage facilities for liquid oxygen at ICBM bases led to adoption of the more effective system of producing fuel directly at the launching sites.

Simulations of various Air Force logistics systems have been made in RAND's Logistics Systems Laboratory. Here men and computers are used to experiment with alternative logistics policies and explore the consequences of changes in maintenance practices, in centralization of support, in information flows, and in management practices, all to the end of developing more efficient logistics systems.

*       *       *

*Economics and Politics*

In 1948, originally at the suggestion of the Joint Chiefs of Staff, RAND began a research program on the economic and military capabilities of the Soviet Union. This continuing research first stimulated and later supplemented government and university research on these topics. Studies have been made on various sectors of the Soviet economy: national income and capital formation; prices, wages, and output; population and the labor force; economic programs, policies, and performance. Studies have also been made of changes in Soviet strategic and military thought, Soviet leadership, Soviet civil defense, the performance of the Soviet system in crisis and disaster situations, and of Soviet techniques for exploiting military power and technological achievements—in space, for example.

Research on Communist China started later and has been 21

carried out on a more modest scale. It has produced reports on national income and product for 1952–1960; the adaptation of Chinese Communist military thinking to the nuclear era; the strategy and tactics of China's foreign policy, and factors leading to China's decision to enter the Korean War; and one study assessed the implications for the United States of a prospective Chinese tactical nuclear capability.

The Corporation has also worked on other aspects of military systems, and the world of conflict and cooperation in which they operate—studies, large and small, of topics as diverse as foreign aid programs, arms control, defense against ballistic missiles, ways of strengthening alliances and improving mutual defenses, operations in crises, the interaction of political and military factors in the conduct of limited war and cold war, weapons and tactics for limited war and counterinsurgency operations, among others.

* * *

*Missiles*
*and*
*Space*

RAND's first studies of space and missile technologies have been mentioned in an earlier section. These and subsequent studies have resulted in a number of significant contributions to space projects, both civil and military. For instance, work begun in 1952 pointed to mass-transfer or ablation-cooling as the preferred way of solving the nose cone re-entry heating problem. Methods to achieve a safe passage of missiles through the earth's atmosphere and that of other planets were studied. By 1956 recovery of a simple satellite of the Vanguard type was thought possible. Next it was shown how a satellite which orbited the moon could be returned to earth. In late 1957 research indicated the feasibility of descent to a selected area on the earth's surface. The Air Force Discoverer program followed early in 1958.

RAND's earliest investigations had shown that satellites could
22  be used as weather-observing platforms, and a detailed report

on this application had been published in 1951. Approaches suggested in this early report were essentially those used for the Tiros weather satellite, developed in 1958 under the direction of the Advanced Research Projects Agency of the Defense Department, and subsequently taken over by the National Aeronautics and Space Administration. The authors of the 1951 report were honored a decade later by the American Meteorological Society for their "pioneering work in the planning of a meteorological satellite." By 1953 RAND's knowledge of the missile and weapon fields indicated that nuclear warheads could be carried by rockets, and could produce a wide enough zone of destruction on impact to more than compensate for their aiming errors. This bore directly on the U.S. decision in 1954 to proceed with the Atlas ICBM program. By then RAND had begun work on ICBM defense studies, with results applicable to the ballistic-missile early-warning system and to the problems, for offense and defense, of ICBM decoys.

In 1957 RAND had considered the Thor-Able rocket (Thor intermediate-range missile with a Vanguard second stage) as a way of obtaining quickly a reconnaissance satellite. New developments in re-entry technology and nuclear warheads suggested that the same launcher could serve as an ICBM, as a back-up to the Atlas program. After a December 1957 recommendation, the program was initiated in January 1958 and a successful first flight was made in July. Happily, the Atlas program was a success, so the Thor-Able was not needed for the operational force.

In 1959 RAND began research on space activities for the National Aeronautics and Space Administration. This work included a broad study of national policy issues arising in a communications satellite system. The study considered many aspects of the problem: satellite technology; economic potential; launch control; ownership and operation; regulation of rates; allocation of radio frequencies; relationship between commercial operation

*Communications Satellite*

23

and military requirements; possible worldwide participation in management and operation; division of costs between users and general public; the sequence of decisions required of the United States Government; the major technical capabilities and advantages and disadvantages of the three main alternative satellite systems—24-hour active, low-altitude active, and passive reflecting. The study pointed out the likely consequences of adopting each of several alternative policy positions.

Late in 1962, when the President appointed an organizing body to lay the groundwork for the Communications Satellite Corporation, a public-private enterprise, RAND was asked by the incorporators of the new organization to bring its earlier research on communications satellites up to date. This was done as part of the research program sponsored by The RAND Corporation with its own funds.

Other RAND space research has included development of computer techniques for calculating trajectories; estimates of the effect of meteorites striking spacecraft or missiles, reducing costs and improving reliability of rocket launches, the international legal and political implications of space activities, problems of lunar and interplanetary exploration, the geomagnetic field and the motion of charged particles, the astronomical constants of the solar system, and comparison of propulsion systems for interplanetary missions. Studies in 1963, made by an astronomer and a mathematician, involve the farthest reaches of space; they show, both by theory and observation, that galaxies come in certain discrete sizes.

*     *     *

Economic Analysis

In 1957 RAND began a study of urban transportation. This included research on the technology of private and mass transportation, present and future patterns of land use, trip-making behavior, government policy affecting land use and transportation requirements, and the development of a general simulation

24

model of land use and transportation. From 1961–1963 this work was supported by a Ford Foundation grant.

In 1953 a study was begun on the technology and economics of water supply, including an appraisal of various means of obtaining fresh water from salt water. The final report showed how the rigorous application of economic principles may produce greater efficiency in water procurement and use. Many of its conclusions were and are at variance with practices governing the use of existing water supplies and the development of new supplies. Another study considered the applicability of systems analysis to water resource development.

In 1959 RAND was asked by The Ford Foundation to assess the applicability of systems analysis to the study of elementary and secondary education in the United States. As a result of this preliminary exploration, the study was continued under the joint sponsorship of The Ford Foundation and RAND. In its second phase, the study dealt with the relations between teacher shortages and salary schedules in the public secondary schools. It argued that a salary schedule offering higher pay to teachers whose specialty was in short supply would be an effective and relatively inexpensive way of alleviating the shortages in the short run, and of balancing teacher supply and demand in the long run. The suggestions in the report have formed the basis of action by a number of school districts throughout the country.

In response to requests from states and municipalities for help with data-processing problems, Corporation-sponsored research was initiated on ways in which modern computing equipment can assist or improve local government processes.

\*　　\*　　\*

As a speaker at the 1957 NATO Conference on Operational Research said, the broad terms of RAND's Air Force contract provide considerable freedom to carry on basic research and [RAND] must be credited with many of the great developments in operations research technique over the past few years.

Such work includes the fields of linear and dynamic programming, game theory, network theory, and the like.

*Mathematics*
Linear programming is a mathematical tool whose development is closely associated with RAND. Here one seeks to optimize some objective while satisfying a collection of constraints, such as minimum costs of production or transportation, maximum profits, maximum ready aircraft, and so on. One finds unexpected connection between problems apparently unrelated. For example, the problem of efficient assignment of targets to aircraft and missiles leads to advances in methods of decentralized planning in a large-scale organization.

Dynamic programming, a mathematical technique originated by a RAND staff member, is, as the *Journal of the Association for Computing Machinery* said, "not only a new branch of analysis but also a powerful new technique in many fields of mathematical application . . . a basic new tool for many kinds of applications of mathematical thinking to the real world, from economics to electrical engineering." Dynamic programming is an approach, by functional equations, to problems that can be phrased in terms of a sequence of decisions, all pointing toward an optimum of some kind: minimum time-to-climb for an aircraft, maximum capacity for a communication network, maximum time in position for a 24-hour satellite with a fixed amount of fuel.

*Theory of Games*
The mathematician von Neumann devised the theory of games to analyze situations in which two or more parties have interests that may be both cooperative and conflicting. RAND has made many contributions to the development of the theory and has applied it to various tactical problems—such as to radar search and prediction, to allocation of defense to targets of unequal value, to missile penetration aids, to the scheduling of

26

missile fire under enemy pindown, to antisubmarine warfare, and to inspection for arms control.

On the other hand, in studies of policy analysis, it is not the theorems that are useful but rather the spirit of game theory and the way it focuses attention on conflict with a live, dynamic, intelligent, and reacting opponent. In military systems, and in the complementary measures of arms control, conflicting as well as cooperative interests must be considered. In time of war we tend to overlook the cooperative interests; in time of peace, the conflicting interests. The conscientious designer of a defense system must consider alternately the defense system and ways in which it might be countered. If he is prudent, he will rely neither on total opposition nor on total cooperation from his opponent. Similarly, in considering arms control agreements it is necessary to think both of control and of possible attempts to evade control. For example, in seeking to determine inspection requirements during the nuclear test-ban negotiations, RAND developed a theory, confirmed in subsequent weapon tests, that described how an underground nuclear blast could be muffled (decoupled, in a cavity, from its surroundings), reducing the seismic signal three hundred fold. This revealed an important technical avenue for possible evasion.

The term "systems analysis" generally includes broader and more difficult problems than those traditionally covered by the terms "operations analysis" or "operations research." The latter terms are often applied to studies of existing systems, or to some tractable facets of a single system, designed to uncover more effective ways to perform specific missions. Systems analysis, on the other hand, refers to the far more complex problem of choice among alternative future systems, where the degrees of freedom and the uncertainties are large, where the difficulty lies as much in deciding what ought to be done as in how to do it.

*Systems Analysis*

The operations researcher uses mathematics or logical analy- 27 sis to find more efficient ways to operate, in situations where the meaning of "more efficient" is fairly clear. The systems analyst, on the other hand, is often faced by problems where the difficulties lie in deciding what ought to be done, what are good objectives and criteria, what, indeed, is the problem. The total analysis is thus a complex and untidy procedure, often with little emphasis on mathematical models, with no possibility of quantitative optimization over the whole problem, and with necessarily great dependence on considered judgments. One of the tools which RAND has found especially useful in such situations is that of operational gaming, or simulation by groups of people—quasi-experimentation, since actual experimentation in the real world is not feasible. The method lays particular emphasis on clarity in problem formulation. It allows the inclusion of qualitative factors. It also provides a means by which scholars in several fields can work together, applying their intuition and advice to common problems. RAND games have dealt, for example, with hypothetical offense and defense force structures for the United States and the Soviet Union over the next decade, with contingencies in the cold war, and with the design and effectiveness of military assistance programs.

\* \* \*

*Computers*    We are at the beginning of a computer revolution, perhaps as profound as the industrial revolution. It is a revolution in which man's intellectual power will be augmented by machines just as the power of his muscles has been. The accomplishments of the last decade in the field of space technology, for example, would have been impossible without the new computers, with their speed and reliability at arithmetic. The essence of the computer is not arithmetic, however, but rather the manipulation of symbols and the processing of information. So far, the organ-
28    izational aspects of the computer and its program, and the infor-

mation processes that it uses, are crude and primitive. RAND has made useful contributions in the past and is trying now to expand further the capabilities of the computer in these directions.

One such study, research in heuristics, concerns the ways in which people perform mental tasks, and then attempts to design machines that can imitate human performance and, hopefully, can learn to improve on it. Such machines need not copy actual human physiology—though other studies do probe in this direction. They may only be formulated as programs in a general-purpose computer. It is useful in such an approach to study tasks that are well defined, well understood, and reasonably difficult, and for which success or failure can be determined. Such definitions lead to an odd assortment of tasks which include, among others, logical calculus, geometry, chess, and checkers.

Another approach seeks to make the computer as useful for processing natural language as it is for handling numbers. Such a capability could greatly increase the worldwide flow of information. It could also be basic to the design of rapid and effective command and control systems, to more efficient processing of technical and strategic intelligence, and to many scientific applications. RAND has attacked the problem of machine translation and other aspects of the automatic processing of language data principally through basic studies of the structure of language itself.

Another study involves the construction of mathematical models of parts and systems of the human body. One good subject for this is the blood, which is a surprisingly complex system. Here the work at RAND has reached such a point that in less than two minutes a computer can accurately calculate the reactions of fifty-six constituents of the blood to such stresses as are imposed by high or low temperature, changes of gas mixtures in the atmosphere, or drastic alterations of the chemical environment. Parallel experiments, performed on the computer

*Mathematics
and
Medicine*

at RAND and in the laboratories of the University of California (Los Angeles) Medical School, suggest that a revolutionary new tool is at hand which can serve medicine both on earth and in space.

\*   \*   \*

*Methodology*     We may conclude with some observations about analysis in general. At its best, analysis can embrace only a part of a broad problem. It obtains no hold at all on some of the subjective elements. Moreover, even before it can organize an understanding of all the objective elements involved, the analysis may become too complex to handle. As RAND alumnus Charles J. Hitch said in a recent speech,

> there will always be considerations which bear on the very fundamentals of national defense which are simply not subject to any sort of rigorous, quantitative analysis. . . . the fact that we cannot quantize such things . . . does not mean that they have no effect on the outcome of a military endeavor—it simply means that our analytical techniques cannot answer every question.

A healthy sense of modesty and realism, then, must surround the use of research as an aid to policy formulation, and RAND is acutely conscious of this.

But to abandon an attempt to be logical about those areas of a problem where the relations of several factors *can* be understood, to give up the attempt to be quantitative about those parts of a problem for which counting and measuring are appropriate, in short, to abandon our efforts at rational analysis, unsatisfactory as these are, would merely uncover the uncomfortable truth that the alternatives also entail analysis—and analysis which may be far more difficult. Reliance upon authority, upon experts and committees, upon verbal arguments, upon intuitive judgments based on experience, still involves a kind of analysis. But now the analysis is both implicit and even more highly oversimplified.

30

Study cannot be a substitute for decision; research cannot play the role of action. Yet analysis can lay bare problems discoverable in no other way. It can stimulate relevant questions; it can provide choices and a market of ideas; it can supply important insights, data, and arguments to the individuals and agencies with policymaking authority and responsibility.

More is involved in analysis than just the collection of information and its manipulation in mathematical models. Asking the right questions, challenging the accepted assumptions, making all assumptions explicit, inventing ingenious alternatives, skillfully interpreting the results of computations, and relating these to the multitude of nonquantifiable factors—all these are parts of the analytic process. Computation is valuable not merely because specific results are established, but more broadly because such computations lead to more and better analysis at the intuitive level. We wish we were sure that all RAND analyses possessed these admirable attributes.

# In the Public Interest

*Publication*

A CONSIDERABLE PART OF THE SPECIALIZED KNOWLEDGE accumulated by the staff of The RAND Corporation through the years is embodied in its publications.

During fifteen years the Corporation has distributed over a million copies of about 7000 RAND publications. Included are 150,000 copies of about 2700 technical papers, prepared for presentation at scientific meetings or for publication in professional journals, and 300,000 copies of about seventy books, issued by commercial publishers and university presses. (See page 41.)

For reasons of security, many of RAND's publications are classified. They go to the military services, to other federal agencies, to industry, and to members of the scientific community with a need-to-know. But a much wider distribution is given to unclassified writings—which compose more than half of the total—through publication in learned journals, through commercially published books, and through limited free distribution of RAND reports. The last category of distribution is achieved largely through deposit libraries—42 in the United States and 7 in foreign countries—each of which has about 2000 RAND publications. Some 800 libraries have RAND's 850-page *Index of Selected Publications*, which lists unclassified items; and they may borrow publications from the deposit libraries.

32      The written word is not the only channel of communication

between RAND and its sponsors and the public. Briefings, lectures, discussion meetings, and symposia have also played an important part in conveying ideas and research results.

Because of its independent, noncompetitive status, RAND has been able to bring together industrial groups on common ground to exchange technical information, and so to enhance productive research. For example, every computer group develops programs and time-saving short cuts. In the early years these were properties either jealously guarded or surreptitiously bootlegged among friendly workers in the field. RAND was able to initiate an overt interchange among computer teams that laid the groundwork for SHARE, a cooperative pooling of programming techniques. It has been estimated that savings of the order of $50 million have been realized by military installations and defense contractors as a consequence of this arrangement. Today, every mass-produced computer in the United States has its own users' cooperative.

In rapidly advancing fields, and especially in those under *Symposia* security restrictions, serious problems of communication exist. An effective way to disseminate information, and to encourage work on neglected problems, is to bring together the principal investigators active in such fields. Symposia, sponsored by RAND, or jointly with the Air Force or other agencies, and attended by military personnel, by industrial researchers, and by university scholars, have dealt with such wide-ranging and varied subjects as the worldwide effects of atomic weapons' fallout, mass-transfer cooling, aerodynamics of the upper atmosphere, manned space stations, protective construction, missile detection and discrimination, linear programming, combinatorial analysis, mathematical biology, simulation of cognitive processes, materials research, the political implications of space, the role of the military in underdeveloped countries, the state of stress in the earth's crust, and lessons learned in counterinsurgency campaigns.

Visitors to RAND average 400 each month. They include 33

military officers, industrial engineers and scientists, university scientists, and statesmen at home and from abroad. To keep in touch with research elsewhere, and to exchange information, approximately 150 members of RAND's staff visit other civilian and military institutions during an.average month.

Techniques conceived or developed at RAND are sometimes presented in the form of courses for military men, and for civilians engaged in related work. To expound the art of systems analysis, together with its advantages and shortcomings, a one-week course was presented several times to Air Force officers and government analysts. RAND has also assisted with the curriculum and has provided faculty for a course in cost analysis techniques at the Air Force Institute of Technology.

*Lectures*     A course of thirty-four lectures covering space topics was presented to 400 key Air Force and Defense Department people soon after the launching of Sputnik I. The lectures were published and used for similar courses at the Air University and the Air Force Institute of Technology. This work was drawn upon in preparing the *Space Handbook* for the House Select Committee on Astronautics and Space Exploration.

RAND staff members are regular lecturers at the National War College, the Industrial College of the Armed Forces, the Air University, the Army War College and Command and Staff College, the Naval War College, and other military service schools. They also lecture at the State Department's Foreign Service Institute and at colleges and universities. Some leave RAND temporarily to accept appointments at universities in this country and abroad, or at such institutions as the Council on Foreign Relations, the Institute for Advanced Study at Princeton, the Center for Advanced Study in the Behavioral Sciences at Palo Alto, and the Harvard Center for International Affairs.

RAND scientists are called upon to serve on numerous scien-
34  tific committees and study groups representing government and

public agencies. These have ranged from advisory bodies concerned with various aspects of national security to committees and panels of the International Geophysical Year and the forthcoming International Years of the Quiet Sun. They have served as field advisors in connection with such negotiations as those for the Korean Armistice, the Geneva Conference on the Discontinuance of Nuclear Weapons Tests, and the Technical Discussions on the Problem of Surprise Attack, also in Geneva.

# In Conclusion

THE MERIT OF RAND HAS DEPENDED ON MANY FACTORS, OF which we may mention a few. Beginning closest to home, it depends principally on the men and women who have worked at RAND.

They seem to have worked predominantly as individuals, with suitable support. From the viewpoint of a researcher with a problem, indeed, RAND hardly looks like a large organization. Certainly it does not look like a "think factory." Rather, it looks like a small group—probably of less than half a dozen persons—who are willing and able to pursue his particular topic of interest as deeply as he can himself, and beyond them a reservoir of at most a few dozen persons whom he feels free to approach for consultation and advice on matters related to his problem. Beyond these, again, there are groups that will provide him with much-needed mechanical services, such as housekeeping, information, computing, costing, and publishing. He is likely to have chosen the problem in which he is involved because it looked especially significant, interesting, and challenging to him, and he and his close colleagues will probably manage that problem, from its cradle to its grave. He will formulate it; then perhaps discuss it with others within RAND, and with persons in government, industry, or the academic community; then he may reformulate it, try to solve it; reformulate it again; and so on, as he strives to include new viewpoints, and new information to meet new objectives, and generally to keep the problem just on the edge of tractability. For research is essentially an untidy process, little resembling the neat image which some conceive to be the "Scientific Method." The investigator may learn only negative things, and pass on to a new problem. If he learns positive things, he may publish his results and possibly spread his message further by stumping for it at a scientific meeting, in industry, or in some government agency.

Hopefully, however outstanding the researcher is, at RAND he finds himself surrounded by people who are his peers; thus he has strong incentives to do his best, particularly since the RAND environment of cooperative research seeks to promote professional comment and criticism throughout the research process, rather than after its completion. By striving to excel in the small community of their colleagues, many RAND researchers have in fact come to excel in the larger community of scholars.

Research management has played an important role in RAND's history. Perhaps its most significant function has been to assemble the elements, to create the necessary organizational arrangements, that have permitted the organization to operate as it has. This challenge is more difficult and subtle than it sounds; the research manager must exercise deliberate self-restraint, for he may be managing best who manages least. The role of Management in program formulation is limited but important. Research that originates principally at the working level will probably constitute an exciting menu. But it is likely to lack balance and exhibit major lacunae when viewed as a program. So Management must add to the menu whatever is needed to make of it a coherent, operative whole.

The role of the Air Force in formally defining the large Project RAND program is both less than most outsiders would expect, and probably more than most insiders suspect. Practically by osmosis—through extensive personal contacts at all levels    37 between Air Force and RAND people—the Corporation becomes aware of problems that are mutually considered to be significant.

The Board of Trustees has contributed wisdom and experience to RAND. There are numerous specific examples of policy guidance from the Board. For example, the charter of the Corporation does not formally restrict the kind of organization for which RAND may do research. But corporate policy has restricted it to government agencies and nonprofit institutions.

Key figures among those responsible for the success of RAND have been the several generations of Air Force officers and government officials and administrators who have shown foresight, and even daring, in supporting the RAND idea, often in the face of strong opposition. The Air Force in particular, but other government sponsors as well, invested in the uncertain promise of dedicated effort in the national interest.

RAND's sponsors would enjoy RAND more, but would value it less, if RAND were always to agree with them. A central fact in the work of RAND, however, is that research and results are never constrained to support particular policies or plans. Inevitably that fact comes to the fore from time to time. The situation is well understood and appreciated at various points in government.

In 1958, in asking RAND to prepare the *Space Handbook* for the use of Congress and the American public, the then Chairman of the House Select Committee on Astronautics and Space Exploration, John McCormack, now Speaker of the House of Representatives, wrote:

> We have had many offers to help from different organizations, and their advice has been beneficial. However, we have come to the conclusion after careful review that The RAND Corporation could make a unique contribution to the cause of public understanding. . . . We particularly like RAND's reputation for independence and integrity.

The 1962 report of the committee chaired by David Bell, then Director of the Bureau of the Budget, which was concerned primarily with the role and the merits of nonprofit organizations engaged in government-sponsored research, stated that the great advantages RAND had to offer were "the detached quality and objectivity of its work."

In 1963, Secretary of Defense McNamara stated that

the larger nonprofit corporations, of which RAND is the most notable, contribute immensely to the success of the Defense Department.

And, on another occasion he said:

In reviewing the work of The RAND Corporation for the Air Force, I consider that they have made some tremendously important contributions in highly technical fields.

Speaking of the annual dollar cost of the RAND contract to the Air Force, Mr. McNamara added, "And for that they receive ten times the value."

In the fifteen years since The RAND Corporation was founded, the United States has been faced with a host of novel and challenging problems in a world that is virtually new. The men and women of RAND have done their best to contribute to the nation's ability to meet these problems.

# Published RAND Books

Akhmanova, O. S., R. M. Frumkina, I. A. Mel'chuk, and E. V. Paducheva. *Exact Methods in Linguistic Research.* Translated from the Russian by David G. Hays and Dolores V. Mohr. Berkeley and Los Angeles: University of California Press, 1963.

Arrow, Kenneth J., and Marvin Hoffenberg. *A Time Series Analysis of Inter-industry Demands.* Amsterdam: North-Holland Publishing Company, 1959.

Baker, C. L., and F. J. Gruenberger. *The First Six Million Prime Numbers.* Madison, Wisc.: The Microcard Foundation, 1959.

Baum, Warren C. *The French Economy and the State.* Princeton, N.J.: Princeton University Press, 1958.

Bellman, Richard. *Adaptive Control Processes: A Guided Tour.* Princeton, N.J.: Princeton University Press, 1961.

Bellman, Richard. *Dynamic Programming.* Princeton, N.J.: Princeton University Press, 1957.

Bellman, Richard. *Introduction to Matrix Analysis.* New York: McGraw-Hill Book Company, Inc., 1960.

Bellman, Richard (ed.). *Mathematical Optimization Techniques.* Berkeley and Los Angeles: University of California Press, 1963.

Bellman, Richard, and Kenneth L. Cooke. *Differential-Difference Equations.* New York: Academic Press, 1963.

Bellman, Richard, and Stuart E. Dreyfus. *Applied Dynamic Programming.* Princeton, N.J.: Princeton University Press, 1962.

Bellman, Richard E., Robert E. Kalaba, and Marcia C. Prestrud. *Invariant Imbedding and Radiative Transfer in Slabs of Finite Thickness*, Modern Analytic and Computational Methods in Science and Mathematics, Vol. 1. New York: American Elsevier Publishing Company, Inc., 1963.

Bergson, Abram. *The Real National Income of Soviet Russia Since 1928*. Cambridge, Mass.: Harvard University Press, 1961.

Bergson, Abram, and Hans Heymann, Jr. *Soviet National Income and Product, 1940–48*. New York: Columbia University Press, 1954.

Brodie, Bernard. *Strategy in the Missile Age*. Princeton, N.J.: Princeton University Press, 1959.

Buchheim, Robert W., and the Staff of The RAND Corporation. *Space Handbook: Astronautics and Its Applications*. New York: Random House, Inc., 1959.

Chapman, Janet G. *Real Wages in Soviet Russia Since 1928*. Cambridge, Mass.: Harvard University Press, 1963.

Dantzig, G. B. *Linear Programming and Extensions*. Princeton, N.J.: Princeton University Press, 1963.

Davison, W. Phillips. *The Berlin Blockade: A Study in Cold War Politics*. Princeton, N.J.: Princeton University Press, 1958.

Dinerstein, H. S. *War and the Soviet Union: Nuclear Weapons and the Revolution in Soviet Military and Political Thinking*. New York: Frederick A. Praeger Inc., 1959.

Dinerstein, H. S., and Leon Gouré. *Two Studies in Soviet Controls: Communism and the Russian Peasant; Moscow in Crisis*. Glencoe, Ill.: The Free Press, 1955.

Dorfman, Robert, Paul A. Samuelson, and Robert M. Solow. *Linear Programming and Economic Analysis*. New York: McGraw-Hill Book Company, Inc., 1958.

Dresher, Melvin. *Games of Strategy: Theory and Applications*. Englewood Cliffs, N.J.: Prentice-Hall, Inc., 1961.

Dubyago, A. D. *The Determination of Orbits*. Translated by R. D. Burke, G. Gordon, L. N. Rowell, and F. T. Smith. New York: The Macmillan Company, 1961.

Edelen, Dominic G. B. *The Structure of Field Space: An Axiomatic Formulation of Field Physics.* Berkeley and Los Angeles: University of California Press, 1962.

Fainsod, Merle. *Smolensk under Soviet Rule.* Cambridge, Mass.: Harvard University Press, 1958.

Ford, L. R., Jr., and D. R. Fulkerson. *Flows in Networks.* Princeton, N.J.: Princeton University Press, 1962.

Gale, David. *The Theory of Linear Economic Models.* New York: McGraw-Hill Book Company, Inc., 1960.

Galenson, Walter. *Labor Productivity in Soviet and American Industry.* New York: Columbia University Press, 1955.

Garthoff, Raymond L. *Soviet Military Doctrine.* Glencoe, Ill.: The Free Press, 1953.

George, Alexander L. *Propaganda Analysis: A Study of Inferences Made from Nazi Propaganda in World War II.* Evanston, Ill.: Row, Peterson and Company, 1959.

Goldhamer, Herbert, and Andrew W. Marshall. *Psychosis and Civilization.* Glencoe, Ill.: The Free Press, 1953.

Gouré, Leon. *Civil Defense in the Soviet Union.* Berkeley and Los Angeles: University of California Press, 1962.

Gouré, Leon. *The Siege of Leningrad, 1941–1943.* Stanford, Calif.: Stanford University Press, 1962.

Gruenberger, F. J., and D. D. McCracken. *Introduction to Electronic Computers.* New York: John Wiley & Sons, Inc., 1963.

Halpern, Manfred. *The Politics of Social Change in the Middle East and North Africa* Princeton, N.J.: Princeton University Press, 1963.

Harris, Theodore E. *The Theory of Branching Processes.* Berlin, Germany: Springer-Verlag, 1963.

Hastings, Cecil, Jr. *Approximations for Digital Computers.* Princeton, N.J.: Princeton University Press, 1955.

Hearle, Edward F. R., and Raymond J. Mason. *A Data Processing System for State and Local Governments.* Englewood Cliffs, N.J.: Prentice-Hall, Inc., 1963.

43

Hirshleifer, Jack, James C. DeHaven, and Jerome W. Milliman. *Water Supply: Economics, Technology, and Policy.* Chicago: The University of Chicago Press, 1960.

Hitch, Charles J., and Roland McKean. *The Economics of Defense in the Nuclear Age.* Cambridge, Mass.: Harvard University Press, 1960.

Hoeffding, Oleg. *Soviet National Income and Product in 1928.* New York: Columbia University Press, 1954.

Hsieh, Alice L. *Communist China's Strategy in the Nuclear Era.* Englewood Cliffs, N.J.: Prentice-Hall, Inc., 1962.

Janis, Irving L. *Air War and Emotional Stress: Psychological Studies of Bombing and Civilian Defense.* New York: McGraw-Hill Book Company, Inc., 1951.

Johnson, John J. (ed.). *The Role of the Military in Underdeveloped Countries.* Princeton, N.J.: Princeton University Press, 1962.

Johnstone, William C. *Burma's Foreign Policy: A Study in Neutralism.* Cambridge, Mass.: Harvard University Press, 1963.

Kecskemeti, Paul. *Strategic Surrender: The Politics of Victory and Defeat.* Stanford, Calif.: Stanford University Press, 1958.

Kecskemeti, Paul. *The Unexpected Revolution: Social Forces in the Hungarian Uprising.* Stanford, Calif.: Stanford University Press, 1961.

Kershaw, Joseph A., and Roland N. McKean. *Teacher Shortages and Salary Schedules.* New York: McGraw-Hill Book Company, Inc., 1962.

Kramish, Arnold. *Atomic Energy in the Soviet Union.* Stanford, Calif.: Stanford University Press, 1959.

Krieger, F. J. *Behind the Sputniks: A Survey of Soviet Space Science.* Washington, D.C.: Public Affairs Press, 1958.

Leites, Nathan. *On the Game of Politics in France.* Stanford, Calif.: Stanford University Press, 1959.

Leites, Nathan. *The Operational Code of the Politburo.* New York: McGraw-Hill Book Company, Inc., 1951.

Leites, Nathan. *A Study of Bolshevism.* Glencoe, Ill.: The Free Press, 1953.

Leites, Nathan, and Elsa Bernaut. *Ritual of Liquidation: The Case of the Moscow Trials.* Glencoe, Ill.: The Free Press, 1954.

44

Lubell, Harold. *Middle East Oil Crises and Western Europe's Energy Supplies.* Baltimore, Md.: The Johns Hopkins Press, 1963.

Markowitz, H. M., B. Hausner, and H. W. Karr. *SIMSCRIPT: A Simulation Programming Language.* Englewood Cliffs, N.J.: Prentice-Hall, Inc., 1963.

McKean, Roland N. *Efficiency in Government through Systems Analysis: With Emphasis on Water Resource Development.* New York: John Wiley & Sons, Inc., 1958.

McKinsey, J. C. C. *Introduction to the Theory of Games.* New York: McGraw-Hill Book Company, Inc., 1952.

Mead, Margaret. *Soviet Attitudes toward Authority: An Interdisciplinary Approach to Problems of Soviet Character.* New York: McGraw-Hill Book Company, Inc., 1951.

Melnik, Constantin, and Nathan Leites. *The House without Windows: France Selects a President.* Evanston, Ill.: Row, Peterson and Company, 1958.

Moorsteen, Richard. *Prices and Production of Machinery in the Soviet Union, 1928–1958.* Cambridge, Mass.: Harvard University Press, 1962.

Newell, Allen (ed.). *Information Processing Language-V Manual.* Englewood Cliffs, N.J.: Prentice-Hall, Inc., 1961.

O'Sullivan, J. J. (ed.). *Protective Construction in a Nuclear Age.* 2 vols. New York: The Macmillan Company, 1961.

The RAND Corporation. *A Million Random Digits with 100,000 Normal Deviates.* Glencoe, Ill.: The Free Press, 1955.

Rush, Myron. *The Rise of Khrushchev.* Washington, D.C.: Public Affairs Press, 1958.

Scitovsky, Tibor, Edward Shaw, and Lorie Tarshis. *Mobilizing Resources for War: The Economic Alternatives.* New York: McGraw-Hill Book Company, Inc., 1951.

Selznick, Philip. *The Organizational Weapon: A Study of Bolshevik Strategy and Tactics.* New York: McGraw-Hill Book Company, Inc., 1952.

Shanley, F. R. *Weight-Strength Analysis of Aircraft Structures.* New York: McGraw-Hill Book Company, Inc., 1952.

45

Smith, Bruce Lannes, and Chitra M. Smith. *International Communication and Political Opinion: A Guide to the Literature.* Princeton, N.J.: Princeton University Press, 1956.

Sokolovskii, V. D. *Soviet Military Strategy.* Translated and annotated by H. S. Dinerstein, L. Gouré, and T. W. Wolfe. Englewood Cliffs, N. J.: Prentice-Hall, Inc., 1963.

Speier, Hans. *Divided Berlin: The Anatomy of Soviet Political Blackmail.* New York: Frederick A. Praeger Inc., 1961.

Speier, Hans. *German Rearmament and Atomic War: The Views of German Military and Political Leaders.* Evanston, Ill.: Row, Peterson and Company, 1957.

Speier, Hans, and W. Phillips Davison (eds.). *West German Leadership and Foreign Policy.* Evanston, Ill.: Row, Peterson and Company, 1957.

Tanham, G. K. *Communist Revolutionary Warfare: The Viet Minh in Indochina.* New York: Frederick A. Praeger Inc., 1961.

Trager, Frank N. (ed.). *Marxism in Southeast Asia: A Study of Four Countries.* Stanford, Calif.: Stanford University Press, 1959.

Whiting, Allen S. *China Crosses the Yalu: The Decision To Enter the Korean War.* New York: The Macmillan Company, 1960.

Williams, J. D. *The Compleat Strategyst: Being a Primer on the Theory of Games of Strategy.* New York: McGraw-Hill Book Company, Inc., 1954.

Wolf, Charles, Jr. *Foreign Aid: Theory and Practice in Southern Asia.* Princeton, N.J.: Princeton University Press, 1960.

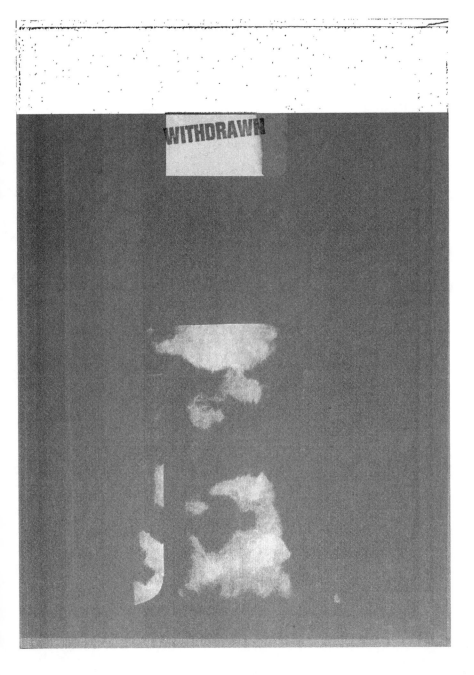

CPSIA information can be obtained
at www.ICGtesting.com
Printed in the USA
BVHW051220170223
658644BV00003BB/109